To mom, dad, grandma, and grandpa –
thank you for encouraging me to reach for the stars.

Visit us on the Web!
www.tinkertoddlers.com

Contact us!
tinkertoddlerbooks@gmail.com

Tinker Toddlers supports early STEM learning. STEM is an acronym for science, technology, engineering, and mathematics. We provide simple explanations about emerging STEM concepts to the littlest learners to help facilitate the absorption of complex details later in life.

Introducing STEM early has shown to improve aptitude in math, reading, writing and exploratory learning in a wide spectrum of topics.

The Solar System!

for KIDS

Dr. Dhoot

Tinker Toddlers®

moon

satellite

airplane

rocket

Look up at the night sky.
What do you see?

Milky Way Galaxy

Andromeda Galaxy

shooting star

Do you see the moon?

We visited there!

Do you see shooting stars?

⭐ These are **meteorites**,
small rocks, metal or ice on fire!

There are lots of stars.

Orion

Libra

Little Dipper

We connect the stars to make imaginary shapes and name them! These are called **constellations**.

Scorpio

Aries

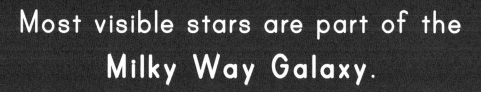

Most visible stars are part of the
Milky Way Galaxy.

This is the
Milky Way Galaxy.

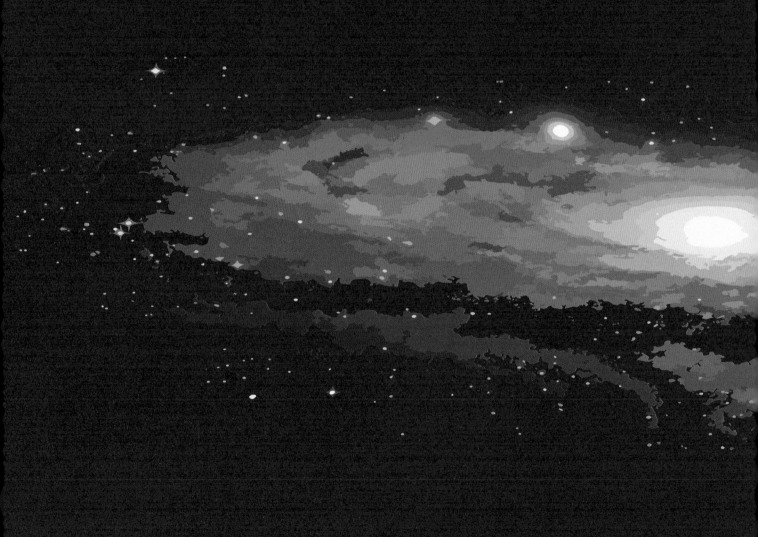

This is our
Solar System.
You live here!

Let's learn about
our Solar System.

During the day, we see the sun.

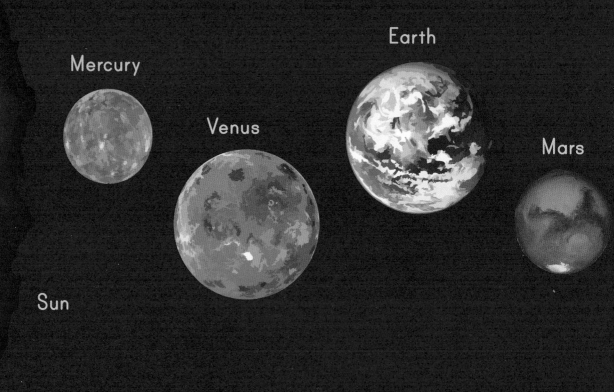

Mercury

Venus

Earth

Mars

Sun

The sun gives light and warms the Solar System.

The sun is the center of our Solar System.

Jupiter

Saturn

Neptune

Uranus

8 planets go around the sun.
Can you count them?

Mercury

is the closest planet to the sun.

◆ This planet goes the *fastest* around the sun.

Venus

can usually be seen at night.

⬠ This planet is the Hottest
and BRIGHTEST.

You are on Earth right now.

Earth has one moon
and beautiful oceans.

We share our planet with many creatures and plants.

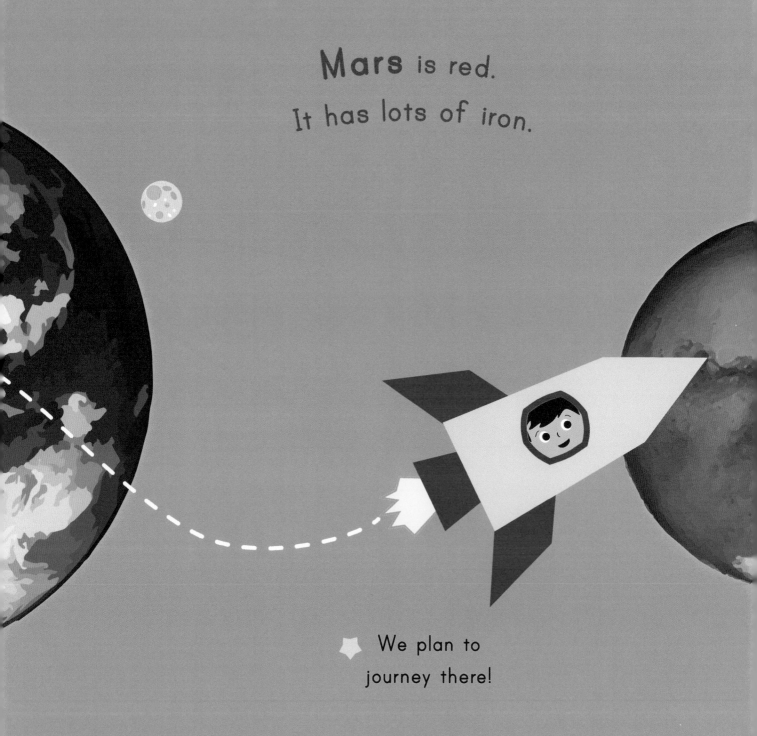

Mars is red.

It has lots of iron.

We plan to
journey there!

Mars has **GIANT** volcanoes.

Curiosity

The
Asteroid belt
is between
Mars and Jupiter.

Asteroids are large rocks that orbit around the sun.

Jupiter is HUGE!

It's the largest planet
that goes around the sun!

Jupiter has a raging storm
that's bigger than Earth!

Jupiter has 79 moons!
That's more than any other
planet in our solar system.

Saturn has beautiful rings.

Its rings are made
of ice and rock!

Uranus is a pretty
pale blue color.

It's tipped with thin rings.

Neptune is the last planet
from the sun! It's very
cold and **dark** there.

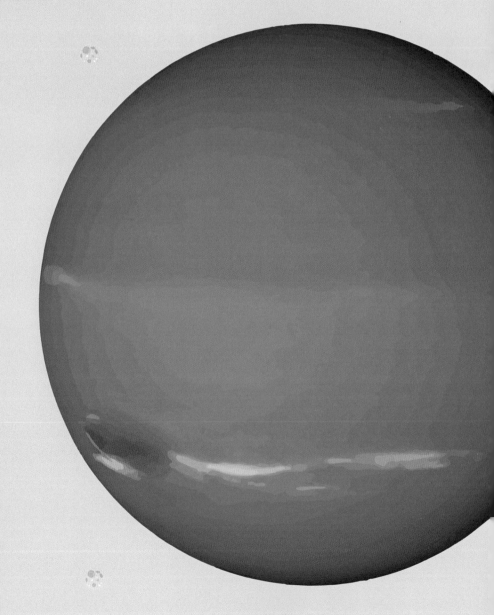

It is the coldest
planet of all!
(on average)

There are lots of other galaxies!

Milky Way Galaxy

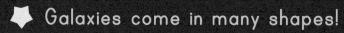 Galaxies come in many shapes!

★ The Andromeda Galaxy can
be seen with the naked eye!

★ The Magellanic Galaxy cloud
can be seen with the naked eye!

All the solar systems, galaxies
and everything in them are
part of the **Universe**.

Our Universe is getting BIGGER!

Where do you want to go?

Dear Reader,

I hope that you enjoyed reading about our solar system! I'm excited to become an interplanetary species, and hope you are too!

Science and technology are evolving rapidly and it can be hard to keep up. I hope you and your little learner(s) enjoyed learning the very basics of our solar system and continue to build your knowledge base.

If you liked this story and want to read more like it, there is a whole series of Tinker Toddlers books on Amazon, just waiting for you.

Best,

Dr. Dhoot

www.TinkerToddlers.com
tinkertoddlerbooks@gmail.com

Tinker Toddlers' Growing Library

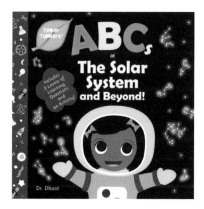

amazon.com/author/drdhoot

tinkertoddlerbooks@gmail.com

Solar System
Certificate

For _____

Tinker Toddlers®

Now you are ready to
explore the Solar System!

Industry experts, scientists, engineers,
parents, and kids contribute much of their time to ensure
Tinker Toddlers is successful at supporting early STEM learning.

To support our efforts, please:

1) go to order history at place of purchase
2) locate product
3) click on "Write a product review"
4) tell us what your favorite part was

Printed in Great Britain
by Amazon

33371504R00023